Published by Sourcebooks, Inc.
P.O. Box 4410, Naperville, Illinois 60567–4410
(630) 961–3900
Fax: (630) 961–2168
www.sourcebooks.com

Originally published in the United Kingdom by Bantam Press,
an imprint of Transworld Publishers

Printed and bound in China.

10 9 8 7 6 5 4 3 2 1

Love is me saying it again on this page.

Waldo Pancake

I love you so much that I went into a shop and bought you a little book about it.

They should make a film about our life together. Minus the watching-TV-on-the-sofa-most-of-the-time bit.

Me

You

society's
pressures

I love it when you use my pockets as a bin for your chocolate wrappers, etc.

Absence makes the choosing what to watch on TV much easier.

Let's paint the town red.

I've just thought this through and realized how much hassle it'd be.

When we have a hug,
I always imagine you're
doing one of those looks
over my shoulder like in
a soap opera, hence me
always hugging you when
we're between two mirrors.

You bring out the **schmaltz** in me.

You had

whatev

you sai

he at
r it was

Would it be weird if I had you stuffed if you died first?

I'm not saying I love your snoring, but the fact that it doesn't make me want to strangle you speaks volumes.

You know when you se

each other's eyes ar

and it makes you wan

Tha

couple looking into
ggling and canoodling
be sick?

'S US.

You bring out the best in me*

*worst might also be brought out.

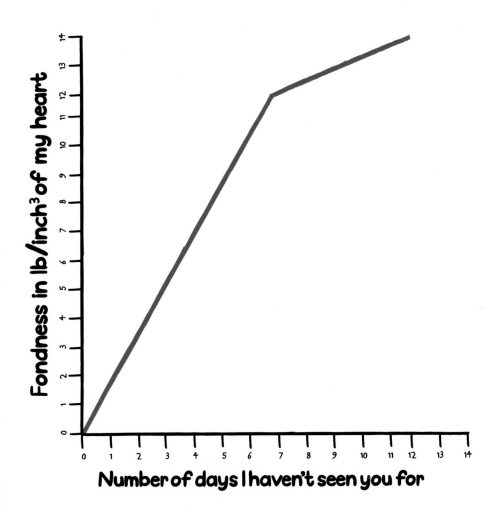

no pressure
there then ——————→

You're my reason for li♥ing.

How ironic would it be if you threw this book at me during a fight.

You a
grea

e the est*

*no scientific proof of this.

I like to imagine us as a really old couple, walking along the street with our canes, holding hands. Although we'll probably have shopping bags in our spare hands. Saying that, we'll be doing our shopping on the internet by then, won't we. Amazing isn't it.

I've read the book*

*what you can say now when subject of love comes up.

You know how couples are always picking bits of fluff off each other's sweaters?

That's why single people are so fluffy.

I love you even more than **me**

I saw one of your socks
on the floor and I felt
the same love for it
that I do for you.

How sad would it be if
I was in a charity shop
after we'd split up or
whatev and I saw this
book on the shelf.

Have you seen those little birds on nature shows that decorate their nests then dance around, trying to attract a mate?

That was me that time when I tidied up my apartment at the beginning of our relationship.

LL

Imagine if "hate" meant "love" and vice versa. I reckon there'd be loads more people saying they loved each other.

People always say "fall in love," which makes me think of someone falling, and how they look terrified.

You know when I'm not listening to what you're saying? That's because I'm too busy thinking about you.

Weird that if we hadn't met I'd be giving this book to someone else.

(Pretend I didn't just think that then write it down and get it printed.)

I only have eyes for you.
And TV.

I had a massive
wave of love
for you today.
It's gone now.

Love is me immediately thinking you've moved whatever it is I'm looking for.

IF I GOT **LOVE** TATTOOED ONTO MY FOREHEAD IN TRIBUTE TO OUR RELATIONSHIP WOULD IT BE WEIRD?

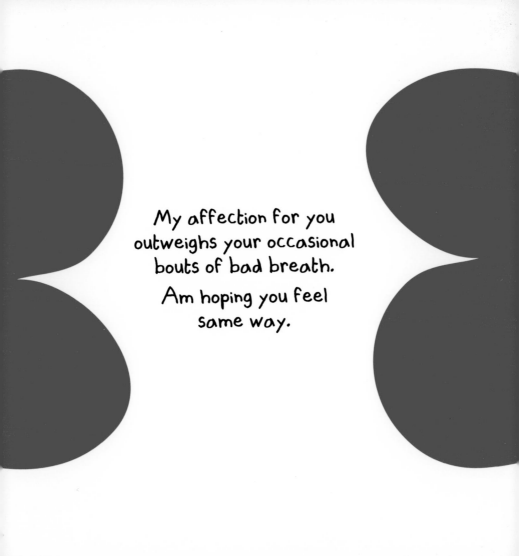

My affection for you outweighs your occasional bouts of bad breath.

Am hoping you feel same way.

Hi, this is the author. I'd just like to point out that it's me writing all this stuff, not the person who bought it for you.

You say tomato,
I go to the fridge
and get you one.

I've contemplated the whole scattering petals thing. Is that good enough for you?

Canoodle,
willoodle.

I love you
to bits.

———→

eye x2	kidney x2
nose	spleen
ear x2	shoulder x2
mouth	neck
leg x2	elbow x2
arm x2	palm x2
nipple x2	bum
thumb x2	thigh x2
fingers x8	etc.
knee x2	
ankle x2	
heart	
liver	
lung x2	

you

My better half →

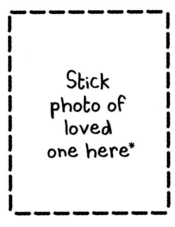

Stick
photo of
loved
one here*

*not gonna happen.

Weird how adding poo to something makes it more lovey-dovey.

Like, "How's my darling poopoo today?"

It just workypoos.

When I put my arm round you, sometimes it's to rest my arm.

Brilliant, another person for me to worry about dying.

You know when you're talking and it's like I'm looking right through you? That's because eyes are the windows to your soul, and I'm staring right at it,

BABY.

Have you seen my book about **VOLE**s? It's like this one, but with V & L swapped round.

If you were a book re♥iew it'd be overwhelmingly positive.

(massive
close-up
of heart)

Completely
and utterly
loved out.

Coming soon

Hate is

buying

book.

me not
you this

You and me'll never end.